MW01196088

IMAGES
of America

FORT MYER

HISTORICAL SITE
DEFENSES OF WASHINGTON
1861 – 1865

FORT WHIPPLE

ON THE HIGH GROUND TO THE NORTHEAST
STOOD FORT WHIPPLE, A BASTIONED EARTHWORK
BUILT EARLY IN 1863 TO SUPPORT THE
ARLINGTON LINE BUILT IN 1861. IT HAD A
PERIMETER OF 640 YARDS AND EMPLACEMENTS
FOR 47 GUNS.
AFTER THE WAR, FORT WHIPPLE WAS MAINTAINED
AS A PERMANENT MILITARY POST. IN 1880, THE
NAME WAS CHANGED TO FORT MYER IN HONOR
OF GENERAL ALBERT J. MYER, FORMER POST COM-
MANDER AND FIRST CHIEF SIGNAL OFFICER OF
THE UNITED STATES ARMY.

ERECTED BY ARLINGTON COUNTY, VIRGINIA, 1965

An Arlington County, Virginia, historical marker is the only publicly visible reminder of the origins of Fort Myer. It's located on US Route 50 near the Henry Gate of Fort Myer. The original fortification was one of more than two dozen forts that comprised the "Arlington Line" and among the 70 forts that surrounded Washington, DC, during the US Civil War. The fort was named Fort Whipple for Brig. Gen. Amiel Weeks Whipple, a Union officer felled by a sharpshooter at the Battle of Chancellorsville in 1863. (Photograph by John Michael.)

ON THE COVER: C Troop of the US Army's 15th Cavalry is mounted, sabers drawn, and ready to lead the charge on the drill field of Fort Myer. The 15th was constituted and organized in February 1901 at the Presidio of San Francisco, California, and immediately sent to the Philippines to quell the insurrection at Mindanao and Luzon in 1902. Upon its return to the United States, the unit was posted to Fort Myer. In the background are the original riding arena on the left and what was then the Post Exchange on the right. (US Library of Congress.)

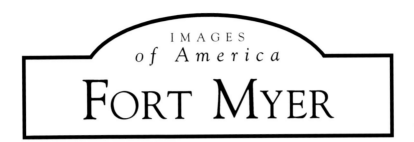

IMAGES
of America

FORT MYER

John Michael

ARCADIA
PUBLISHING

Copyright © 2011 by John Michael Kupik
ISBN 978-0-7385-8735-6

Published by Arcadia Publishing
Charleston, South Carolina

Printed in the United States of America

Library of Congress Control Number: 2010936703

For all general information, please contact Arcadia Publishing:
Telephone 843-853-2070
Fax 843-853-0044
E-mail sales@arcadiapublishing.com
For customer service and orders:
Toll-Free 1-888-313-2665

Visit us on the Internet at www.arcadiapublishing.com

This book is dedicated to my mother, Josephine A. Kupik—thank you for all you have done. It's also dedicated to all the US Army soldiers who are serving and who have served at Fort Myer over the years—you have made this book possible. Thank you for your service.

This is a typical scene on Fort Myer's Summerall Parade Field, whether it is a change of command, a retirement ceremony, or a dignitary's arrival or departure. In the foreground are the guns of the Presidential Salute Battery, while the companies of the 3rd Infantry Regiment—the Old Guard—pass in review along the left of the photograph. Two music units are on the field: the Fife and Drum Corps (in Colonial uniforms) and the US Army Band–"Perishing Own." . Along the hedges in the top center are the soldiers and horses of the Caisson Platoon. (The Old Guard Museum.)

CONTENTS

ACKNOWLEDGMENTS

A book of this kind is a team effort, though one person's name may appear on the front cover. Reaching out, I had a fantastic team that came together that aided in exploring, researching, and preparing this work. So many people and organizations played a key role in its success. Thank you all for your help and support.

A special thank you goes out to Kim Bernard Holien of the Fort Myer History Office for his knowledge, guidance, and the great resources about this historic post. Kirk Heflin and Lea F. Davis of the Old Guard Museum provided insight and access to some great resources of the US Army's 3rd Infantry Regiment. M.Sgt. Michael Parnell, historian of the US Army Band, provided key information that filled in the blanks and provided some great images. Michael Robert Patterson's website, www. ArlingtonCemetery.net, is a repository that provided key facts not found elsewhere. A special thanks goes to Donna Tabor, historian for XVIII Airborne Corps of the US Army, for the insight on "Rodney." I would like to thank Holly Reed and the staff at the National Archives and Records Administration in College Park, Maryland, for their assistance in finding the gems hidden among the US Army Signal Corps collection and helping me navigate the wonders of their resources. The Library of Congress provided many images that were invaluable. I also thank Maj. Gen. Karl R. Horst, commanding general of the Military District of Washington, and Col. Carl R. Coffman, garrison commander of Joint Base Myer–Henderson Hall for their assistance. To three of my advisors/mentors—Col. Charles W. Norton Jr., USA (Ret.), Lt. Col. William Lee Yarborough, USA (Ret.), and Lt. Col. Wallace Johnson, USA (Ret.)—thank you for the guidance, insights, and encouragements over the years. I would have never reached this point without all of you. And thank you to fellow author Gerard Devlin for his suggestions, insights, and tips. To Col. John H. Crerar, USA (Ret.), and Virginia Norton for reading the manuscript and offering their suggestions, comments, and corrections, a special thank you. Finally, to my publisher, Maggie Bullwinkel, and editor, Elizabeth Bray, a special thank you for your patience, guidance, and assistance to bring this all to reality.

Images in this volume appear courtesy of Joint Base Myer–Henderson Hall History Office (first known as Fort Myer History Office [FMHO]); the Old Guard Museum (TOGM); the US Army Band (TUSAB); US National Archives and Records Administration, primarily the US Army Signal Corps collection (NARA); the US Library of Congress (LOC); and the book *In the Company of WACS* by Elna Hilliard Grahn (ICW).

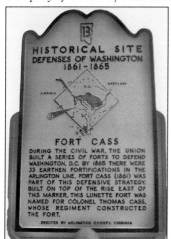

An Arlington County, Virginia, historical marker located on Route 50 shows where a lunette named Fort Cass was built in 1861 within the original 1,100 acres of the Custis-Lee estate. It served as the first line of defense of Washington and was part of the growing Arlington Line—the chain of fortifications that protected the capital from the west. This marker is the only reminder of this notable piece of Civil War history. Present-day Fort Myer includes the land upon which Fort Cass stood. (Photograph by John Michael.)

INTRODUCTION

At Fort Myer today, the history-makers are the US Army's 3rd Infantry Regiment, the "Old Guard;" the US Army Band, "Pershing's Own;" and Headquarters Company of the US Army. Yet Fort Myer's history goes back all the way to the US Civil War. Built in June 1863, it was first named Fort Whipple after Maj. Gen. Amiel Weeks Whipple, who was killed in the battle of Chancellorsville in May 1863. Some say that the location was chosen because that is where the general ordered an observation balloon launched to spy on the Confederates. The area of the present-day installation also includes where Fort Cass, a lunette, was built in August 1861 as the first line of defense and part of the Arlington Line.

On April 12, 1861, the Confederates attacked Fort Sumter, and the US Civil War began. On May 24, 1861, Union troops crossed the Potomac and commanded the high ground surrounding and including the Custis-Lee mansion. After the defeat at Bull Run, given the closeness of the Confederates, Union general George B. McClellan became concerned about the safety of the nation's capital. Although several forts were constructed in early 1861—the first at the two bridges that crossed the Potomac, Fort Jackson at Long Bridge and Fort Haggerty at Aqueduct Bridge—additional fortifications were planned and built. These included several lunettes such as Fort Cass, which was carved from the acreage of the original Custis-Lee estate.

In 1862, Maj. Gen. John Gross Barnard was named chief engineer of the Army of the Potomac. He has also been called the "Father of the Defenses of Washington, DC." General McClellan conceived where to place the capital's defenses, and Major General Barnard designed and oversaw the construction. By the end of the war, a network of nearly 70 fortifications and over 90 batteries would be built to surround and defend the US capital. Around each fort and battery, the land was clear-cut for two miles in all directions to provide a clear line of sight and fire for the artillery. Most of the wood collected from the clear-cutting was used to construct these military compounds. The forts were earthworks with bombproofs and very few permanent buildings.

Upon inspection of the defenses, it was determined that additional fortifications were needed. In augmenting the Arlington Line that was built in 1861, several fortifications were added, one of them on Arlington Heights to redouble the presence of Fort Cass. This was Fort Whipple, which was completed in June 1863. Facing west, it stood on the high ground to the northeast, a bastioned earthwork. It had a perimeter of 658 yards and emplacements for 43 guns.

From July 1861 to October 1862, Maj. Gen. Amiel Weeks Whipple, the fort's namesake, was involved with the defenses of Washington, ultimately as a brigadier general commanding a division of volunteers headquartered at the Custis-Lee mansion. On August 28, 1861, he ordered a balloon aloft to survey the Confederates from a spot where the fortification bearing his name would be built. General Whipple died in Washington on May 7, 1863. President Lincoln attended his funeral and said that he was there as a friend of the family and not as president of the United States. The president not only gave his autographed photograph to the widow, but he gave a presidential appointment to the older son of his friend—as referenced in a note found on page 15 of this book. After Lincoln was assassinated, another note was found on his desk asking his successor, if anything happened to him, to appoint the younger son of General Whipple to Annapolis. This was duly done by Pres. Andrew Johnson.

The first occupants of the fort belonged to the 14th Massachusetts Heavy Artillery Regiment under the command of Lt. Col. L.P. Wright. In July 1864, Lt. Col. Ranald S. Mackenzie was promoted to colonel; he became the commander of the garrison and of the 2nd Connecticut Heavy Artillery Regiment. Gen. Ulysses S. Grant proclaimed that Mackenzie was the most promising officer of the Army. Mackenzie would go on to command the famed "Buffalo Soldiers" of the 24th Infantry and ultimately achieve the rank of brevet brigadier general.

When the Civil War ended, the fortifications around Washington, DC, were abandoned. Only Fort Whipple would survive to the present day. In 1881, it was renamed for the US Army's first signal officer, Maj. Gen. Albert J. Myer. The installation was the first headquarters of the US Army's Signal Corps School.

As the "last one standing," Fort Myer is still an active duty US Army post today that has the distinction of hosting many unique events and historic firsts. Names such as Myer, Sheridan, Barnard, Greely, Henry, Hatfield, Wainwright, Joyce, and Patton have contributed greatly to molding the Arlington Heights acres that have become present-day Fort Myer. Among them are the beginnings of military aviation, the first aviation fatality, a showcase for the US Army Cavalry (both cavalry regiments of the famed Buffalo Soldiers had troopers who were posted here), the first location of "The Three Sisters" (three radio towers erected by the US Navy, one 600 feet and the other two 450 feet tall, that were the first wireless communications towers, built in 1913), the Society Circus, the first application of the telephone, and origin of the National Weather Service. Gen. George S. Patton Jr. would especially leave his mark on Fort Myer, since he was posted here four times during his career: the first from 1911 to 1913, the second from 1920 to 1922, the third from 1932 to 1935, and the fourth from 1938 to 1940, when he was both post commander and commander of the 3rd Cavalry.

In 1883, Gen. Philip H. Sheridan considered Fort Myer to be a strategic location to continue to defend the capital and also showcase the US Army's cavalry. By an act of Congress in 1886, Fort Myer was redesignated as a military station. General Sheridan petitioned the secretary of war to establish it as a cavalry post. The Signal Corps School moved out, and the 6th Cavalry under the command of Maj. James Biddle moved in to occupy the post and defend Washington. It was formally designated a cavalry post in July 1887 with Maj. Louis H. Carpenter as post commander. As the 20th century approached, several cavalry regiments would rotate through the post, including the 5th, 9th, 4th, and 3rd. By this time, several permanent buildings were authorized and built, including the commanding officer's quarters, a hospital, and other officers' quarters—all of which were initially wooden structures. For the sake of safety, during the 1890s, the wooden buildings were replaced with brick ones, and new buildings appeared, including a riding arena in 1893 and the Post Exchange and Quarters One in 1899.

The next era in the history of Fort Myer was when man took to the skies. Lighter-than-air balloons were used quite well during the US Civil War, and the Signal Corps continued their use within the weather service. The post had its own "balloon barn." Yet on the horizon were new and exciting discoveries: rigid airships—dirigibles—and the first heavier-than-air military flight. Despite sustaining injuries in a 1908 plane crash that caused aeronautics' first military fatality, Orville Wright returned to Fort Myer with his brother, Wilbur, in July 1909, and the US Army took to the air. Later, these services moved to College Park, Maryland.

The 11th Cavalry was constituted on February 2, 1901, in the regular Army and was organized on March 11, 1901, at Fort Myer. The regiment was almost immediately sent to the Philippines and saw service there from 1901 to 1904.

Within cavalry and field artillery units, the Army moved by horse until World War II. Based on the need to provide quality animals to the troops, Congress authorized the Remount Service in 1908 and developed three remount depot across the country. The depot at Front Royal, Virginia, built in 1911, supplied Fort Myer. The second was at Fort Reno, Oklahoma, and the third was at Fort Keogh, Montana. By the height of World War I, 39 remount depots dotted the United States. However, the need for animals diminished greatly by World War II as the Army mechanized. By 1948, the Army's Remount Service was disbanded, although it would leave a positive lasting impact on the horse industry. The depot at Front Royal eventually became a research facility of the Smithsonian Institution.

During World War I, part of the post was devoted to trench warfare as taught by the French. In 1917, training was completed for the first class of the Reserve Officers' Training Corps at Fort Myer. The installation was the training location for many Army officers who headed "over there" to fight in the Great War. Afterward, the 3rd Cavalry returned from the war for an extended stay at Fort Myer. In the nearly two decades that it was there, it was the defense of the capital, provided ceremonial support around the District and within Arlington National Cemetery, and provided entertainment for the residents and politicians of Washington, DC. As conceived by George S. Patton Jr., the soldiers performed with the Society Circus. The troops' equestrian skills, honed by repeated drills and the wonderful facilities of Fort Myer, allowed them to represent the United States in the Olympics and to field polo teams that competed with other military installations or civilian teams.

As World War II began, the United States anticipated being drawn into the battle, and Fort Myer became an induction and training location. The Pentagon was being built near the Custis-Lee estate. The flatland near the Potomac River had been known as Arlington Farms. The US Department of Agriculture used the acreage for experimental growing of grains, grasses, and other crops. As the nation prepared for war, the land was requisitioned by the US War Department. The northern acreage remained Arlington Farms, and housing was built for women who worked in Washington, DC. The south acreage first became Arlington Cantonment as additional troops were brought in and housed in temporary quarters—tents. Ultimately barracks and other support buildings were built to house soldiers of what would become Headquarters Company of the US Army and troops from the newly established Women's Army Corps (WAC)—initially called the Women's Army Auxiliary Corps (WAAC). The area was later designated as Fort Myer's South Post.

When the 3rd Cavalry left Fort Meyer in February 1942, they headed south to Fort Oglethorpe, Georgia, then onto Fort Benning, Georgia and finally at Fort Gordon, Georgia they were mechanized. The ceremonial duties then fell upon the machine gun troop of the 10th Cavalry Regiment and a ceremonial company from the remaining soldiers within the Military District of Washington, which was organized to provide support for all the events and final honors at Arlington National Cemetery. When the 3rd US Infantry Regiment, "the Old Guard," was reactivated after World War II, the members of the ceremonial company became the first soldiers in the regiment. The 10th Cavalry would head west in 1949, leaving the Old Guard to both defend the capital and provide the necessary ceremonial support.

The adjutant general, Otto Johnson, issued a proclamation on December 10, 1941, that the provost marshal general should establish what was then known as the Military Police School at Fort Myer, Virginia. The staff and faculty were not to exceed 29 officers, 31 enlisted men, and 28 civilians, and the 703rd MP Battalion was to administer and operate the school.

The Military Police School was established at Arlington Cantonment, Fort Myer, Virginia, on December 19, 1941, but was not in full operation until after February 1, 1942. On January 14, 1942, the name of the school was changed to the Provost Marshal General School. The course of instruction, including basic training for future military policemen, was a five-week course, increased to 13 weeks in May 1942. The school had four departments: Military Law, Traffic Control, Police Methods, and Criminal Investigation.

Since 1942, Fort Myer has been the home of the US Army Band—"Pershing's Own." They were deployed during the war to keep the soldiers' morale high, with the funeral band remaining on Fort Myer to provide support for final honors in Arlington National Cemetery. After World War II, the US Army Band returned home to Fort Myer, and the band was awarded a campaign streamer for its colors. The funeral band continued its ceremonial support within Arlington National Cemetery. Additional segments were added to the band, including the US Army Band Chorus.

It was April 6, 1948, one of the last "Army Day" celebrations, when the 3rd US Infantry—"The Old Guard"—was reactivated on the steps of the US Capitol, it has become the US Army's ceremonial regiment. Also called the "Escort to the President," this regiment continues its stay at Fort Myer. The soldiers of this regiment have a dual mission: providing defense for the National Capital Region—they hone their tactical skills repeatedly—and delivering ceremonial support for Washington, DC, events such as presidential inaugurations, dignitary arrivals, and one of its most respectful and solemn: final honors support duty at Arlington National Cemetery. This regiment also provides the sentinels at the Tomb of the Unknown Soldier. The elite units within the regiment complement their outstanding execution. These include the Caisson Platoon, the Presidential Salute Battery, the Continental Color Guard, the US Army Drill Team, the Old Guard Fife and Drum Corps, and the Commander-in-Chief's Guard.

Fort Myer has also been home to US Army officers who would continue to rise to acting secretary of the Army (Gen. Gordon R. Sullivan) or even the first chairman of the Joint Chiefs of Staff (Gen. Omar Nelson Bradley), or who rose from the military to become president of the United States (Dwight D. Eisenhower), secretary of state (Colin Powell), and secretary of veterans affairs (Eric Ken Shinseki).

The intent of this work is to provide a historical overview of Fort Myer through many original photographs combined with a great and exciting story of this historic US Army post's first 100 years—from the 1860s to the 1960s. It displays the evolution of this national landmark and treasure over time: the buildings, the people, and events that have had an impact on the United States and the world. Since its beginnings, Fort Myer has been the epicenter of events. In this book, for the first time, images for many of those milestones are presented in one work. It is an honor and serendipitous that the first book about Fort Myer is released just as we're entering the sesquicentennial commemoration of the Civil War from 2011 through 2015.

That said, given the deep history of this US Army post, the hardest decision has been what to include that would provide highlights and depth to spur further research on the reader's part. Any omission or error is not intentional, but the fault falls upon the author alone. This is a groundbreaking work, since no other works of any significance with a focus on Fort Myer, Virginia, have been discovered to date. The author welcomes your feedback and suggestions at the book's website, www.Historic-FortMyer.com. You'll also find among other things on the website the following: a glossary, an index, a bibliography, and suggested additional reading.

One

DEFEND THE CAPITAL

During the Civil War, the Union built a series of forts to defend Washington, DC. By 1865, there were 21 earthen fortifications in the Arlington Line. Maj. D.P. Woodbury was the engineer who designed and oversaw the building of the entire Arlington Line.

The Arlington Line consisted of Battery Garesche, Fort Reynolds, Fort Barnard, Fort Berry, Fort Richardson, Fort Albany, Fort Scott, Fort Runyon, Fort Jackson, Fort Craig, Fort McPherson, Fort Tillinghast, Fort Cass, Fort Whipple, Fort Woodbury, Fort Morton, Fort Corcoran, Fort Haggerty, Fort Bennett, Fort Strong, and Fort C.F. Smith. Reflecting upon the efforts expended to strengthen Washington's Civil War defenses, Lt. Col. Barton S. Alexander, chief engineer of the capital's defenses in 1865, wrote: "It seems to me, after our experience during this rebellion, that a wise foresight will not permit us to allow the seat of government to become again entirely defenseless."

Gen. Winfield Scott had a 47-year career with the US Army and commanded military forces in many campaigns and wars, including the War of 1812 and the Mexican-American War. He devised a plan to defeat the Confederacy in the Civil War called the "Anaconda Plan," an outline strategy for subduing the seceding states. General Scott is the one who would give the name "Old Guard of the Army" to the 3rd Infantry Regiment. The regiment participated in eight battles, including the final bayonet assault on the fortress of Chapultepec. On September 14, 1847, the 3rd Infantry was the lead regiment as the US Army made its grand entrance into Mexico City. As the troops passed in review during the parade, General Scott is reputed to have turned to his staff and said "Gentlemen, take off your hats to the Old Guard of the Army." As commanding general of the Army, his successor was Gen. George B. McClellan. (NARA.)

Gen. Robert Edward Lee, a graduate of West Point, was the engineer of such coast artillery forts as Fort Pulaski, Fort Monroe, and Fort Carroll. He was offered the post of general of the Union Army but held his allegiance to the commonwealth of Virginia, his family, and his home. The 1,100-acre Custis-Lee estate, where he lived for 30 years, would eventually become home to Fort Myer and Arlington National Cemetery. (NARA.)

Gen. George B McClellan assumed command of the US Army from Winfield Scott and implemented Scott's plan to win the Civil War, the Anaconda Plan. McClellan also devised a plan to defend the capital through a series of fortifications and artillery batteries that would surround Washington, DC, and award it the distinction of the most fortified city during the war. (LOC.)

When the taxes weren't paid on the Custis-Lee estate, the 1,100 acres were confiscated by the US government and put under the control of the quartermaster general of the Army, Montgomery C. Meigs. He established what would become Arlington National Cemetery when he proposed that part of the property—specifically, the garden of Mary Anna Custis-Lee, Robert E. Lee's wife—be used as a burying place for the Civil War dead. (NARA.)

Gen. John Gross Barnard planned and executed the building of the fortifications and batteries after General McClellan decided where to place them. He would eventually become known as Father of the Defenses of Washington and would design Fort Whipple. (NARA.)

Maj. Gen. Amiel Weeks Whipple was a native of Massachusetts. He was first assigned to the defense of Washington. His headquarters was the Custis-Lee mansion, Arlington House. He ordered an observation balloon aloft at the spot where a fort would be built that would carry his name. Shot at the battle of Chancellorsville on the Rappahannock River, he later died from his wound. (LOC.)

Within a week of the death of General Whipple, this Executive Mansion note from Abraham Lincoln, a very rare find, was written because of the relationship which had developed between the president and General Whipple and the president's fondness for the general's sons. While Whipple was commander of the defenses of Washington, his headquarters was at Arlington House. The president would drive across the Potomac and often have lunch there, which included lemonade. Lincoln would get the updates from the general with his arms wrapped around Whipple's two sons. It was later learned that in addition to this note to General Totten making the presidential appointment of William Whipple to the US Military Academy, another note had been written by Lincoln that assured that Whipple's younger son would be appointed to the US Naval Academy if Lincoln should not be able to make the appointment. (Both NARA.)

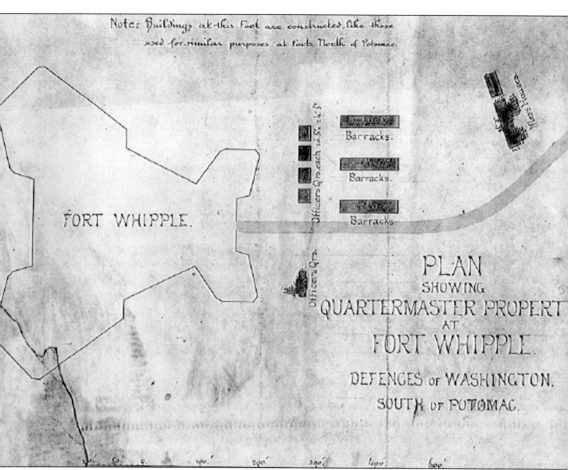

Note: Buildings at this Fort are constructed like those used for similar purposes at forts North of Potomac.

FORT WHIPPLE.

Officers Qrs.each 25 ft.25 ft.

Barracks.

Barracks.

Barracks.

Officers Qrs.

PLAN
SHOWING
QUARTERMASTER PROPERT
AT
FORT WHIPPLE.

DEFENCES OF WASHINGTON.

SOUTH OF POTOMAC.

Built in 1863, these plans for Fort Whipple have the fort facing west. It augmented Fort Cass, which was built in 1861 and is still part of Fort Myer. The plan shows that the commanding officer's quarters were nearest to the entrance of the bastion earthworks on the south side of the fort. (NARA.)

This is the front of the Headquarters Building of Fort Whipple. It is one of the few photographs taken of this historic fort. It is unclear why the black bunting is draped over the doorway and the windows. The image was captured after the death of President Lincoln in June 1865. (LOC.)

Looking at the interior of Fort Whipple, these batteries in the fort faced to the northeast and originally were manned by the soldiers of the 14th Massachusetts Heavy Artillery. Other artillery units that were posted to the fort during the Civil War included heavy artillery from Ohio, Connecticut, New York, and Pennsylvania. (LOC.)

This is the western side of Fort Whipple looking west. Visible is the extensive clear-cutting that was done both to gather wood to construct the defenses of Washington and to provide the artillery a clear line of fire two miles in all directions. (LOC.)

Taken at Fort Corcoran, this images shows a typical gun emplacement with soldiers and a stack of grapeshot next to the gun. Most of these soldiers are officers who have just posed for the photographer. Note the soldier leaning on the wheel of the gun with his arm in a sling. The role of artilleryman was very hazardous and prone to injury from any number of things, including an exploding cannon and movement of the carriage, since the recoilless version had not yet been invented. (NARA.)

Col. Ranald Slidell "Bad Hand" Mackenzie attended the US Military Academy and graduated first in the class of 1862. He commanded Fort Whipple in 1864 while attached to the 2nd Connecticut Heavy Artillery volunteers and was considered one of the most promising officers by Gen. Ulysses S. Grant. Mackenzie would later fight in the Indian Wars, commanding the 24th Infantry Regiment. (FMHO.)

Here the officers of the 3rd US Infantry Regiment pose for a group photograph. The regiment fought in the Battle of First Manassas (Bull Run) and would also be at the signing of the surrender at Appomattox Courthouse. The oldest infantry regiment in the US Army was given the name "Old Guard of the Army" by Gen. Winfield Scott. The regiment would in later years become the ceremonial unit of the US Army, stationed at Fort Myer. (LOC.)

During the US Civil War, communication was a key to understanding the movements and positions of troops. Here is a typical lookout and signal station with the wig-wag flag flown at the top of the tower. Other lookouts were placed on top of buildings within forts and downtown Washington, DC. The wig-wag signaling method was designed by Gen. Albert J. Myer. It consisted of one flag and a method that resembled Morse Code. (LOC.)

Two

A New Name and the Signal Corps School

After the Civil War, Fort Whipple was still federal property, and artillery units continued to occupy the fort until 1868. The Signal Corps School moved in early in 1869, and the first permanent construction began. In 1872, Congress decided to make it a permanent installation.

Gen. Albert J. Myer was appointed chief signal officer in 1866. He began a Signal Corps school in his office in downtown Washington, DC. When that space became too crowded, he sought other space for the school, first at Fort Greble. He ultimately chose Fort Whipple because of its location on high ground and its considerably larger size. Here the school would stay for nearly two decades.

And the developments began: the first ever telephone line was strung between Fort Whipple and the War Department downtown relatively soon after Alexander Graham Bell applied for a patent. Space was abundant on post, which allowed other project-testing to occur. Besides the wig-wag signaling method, the heliograph—a signaling technique using mirrors and the sun—was developed. It later proved very useful in the US Southwest and was used until the beginnings of World War I. In 1870, the National Weather Bureau was formed by the Signal Corps on Fort Myer, with stations around the country reporting their "probables." This was another contribution made by General Myer.

General Myer died in 1880, and the Signal Corps lost its most active proponent. In his honor, Fort Whipple was renamed Fort Myer. Brig. Gen. William Hazen took command of the Signal Corps for a brief time. When he assumed command, permanent buildings, though constructed of wood, were already in place.

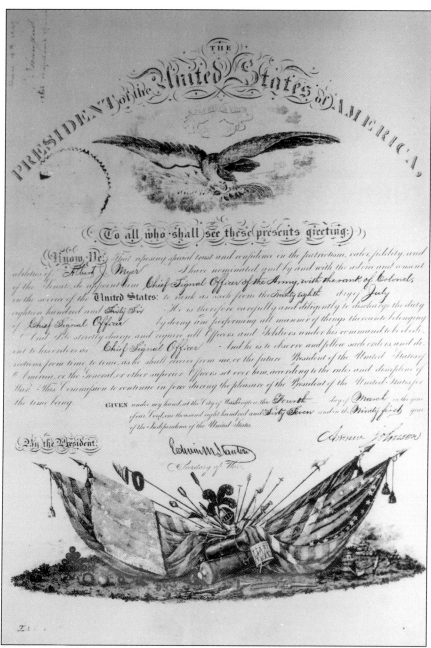

This is the order appointing Gen. Albert J. Myer the US Army's chief signal officer. In the 1850s, Maj. Albert J. Myer, a surgeon by training, developed a system using left or right movements of a flag or torch or lantern at night. Myer's system used a single flag, waved back and forth in a binary code conceptually similar to the Morse Code of dots and dashes. This is sometimes called the "wig-wag" method of signaling, or "wig-wagging." More mobile than previous means of optical telegraphy—it only required one flag and a six-to-eight-foot platform on which to stand the signal corpsman—this code was used extensively by signal troops on both sides in the American Civil War. Confederate lieutenant Edward Porter Alexander used wig-wag in battle at the First Battle of Bull Run in 1861. General Myer also organized the National Weather Service in 1870. (FMHO.)

Gen. Albert J. Myer was trained as a surgeon. He was intrigued by communication and sought ways to communicate over long distances. In 1850, he invented the wig-wag signaling method, which employed just one flag—at night it was complemented by a torch. From the method he originated, the crossed signal flags and torch make up the US Army Signal Corps insignia. (FMHO.)

One of the first permanent buildings on Fort Whipple, built in 1876, was the wood-frame Commanding Officer's Quarters. It overlooked the city of Washington, DC. Unlike on other forts, the first parade field was in back of these quarters. (NARA.)

In the 1870s, the US Army built a 12-bed hospital and bridge, also of wood construction. The bridge spanned a ravine that was later filled as further development occurred at the post. (NARA.)

Also constructed before 1880 were the quarters on Officers' Row, which faced towards the east with a very scenic view of Washington, DC, and the Washington Monument. Despite officers' quarters, however, the fort still faced a shortage of barracks and stables. (NARA.)

Gen. William Babcock Hazen, a West Point graduate of the class of 1855, was the second chief Signal Corps officer. During his command, Adolphus Greely and several others were stranded at Ellesmere Island while on an expedition to the Arctic. Hazen sent a team to rescue the expedition despite political protests. (FMHO.)

On November 1, 1883, Philip H. Sheridan succeeded William T. Sherman as commanding general of the US Army, and he held that position until shortly before his death. He was promoted on June 1, 1888, to the rank of general in the regular army (the rank was titled "general of the Army of the United States," by act of Congress). He would turn Fort Myer into a showplace for the cavalry. (NARA.)

General of the Army Philip H. Sheridan was one of the first flag officers to be laid to rest in Arlington National Cemetery. His final resting place is on the south side of the Custis-Lee mansion overlooking the city of Washington, DC. It's his way of perpetually standing in defense of the capital. (LOC.)

Three

The Cavalry, the Signal Corps Returns, and World War I

On July 6, 1887, Fort Myer was designated a cavalry post by General Order No. 42 from Gen. Philip H. Sheridan. Louis Henry Carpenter became the Fort Myer commander while commanding the 6th Cavalry. After the Civil War, he had been promoted to captain, US Regular Army. His first assignment was to recruit African Americans for two new cavalry units—the famed 9th and 10th US Cavalry, which came to be known as the "Buffalo Soldiers." Afterwards, as commander of Troop H, 10th US Cavalry, he saw continuous Western frontier service from 1866 to 1870. He would earn a Medal of Honor and be promoted to brigadier general.

As the 20th century approached, wood-frame buildings disappeared and were replaced with new buildings constructed of brick. The 1890s saw an aggressive building effort with many buildings constructed: four stables, two NCO quarters, two enlisted men's barracks, two officers' quarters (on Lee and Jackson Avenues), the riding arena, a new hospital, a guardhouse, a headquarters (later named Patton Hall and the Officers' Club), and a new commanding officer's residence: Quarters One.

The cavalry on post was complemented by a field artillery unit. This combination of forces defended the capital and responded to the ceremonial needs. The Buffalo Soldiers from Troop K of the 9th Cavalry were stationed at Fort Myer from 1891 to 1894 after long, arduous frontier service.

As the 1900s began, a new West Point graduate would come to Fort Myer for the first of his four tours here. George S. Patton Jr. was assigned as a leader of a machine gun platoon in the 15th Cavalry and made his first mark designing a new sword the US Army would adopt: nearly 40,000 of these M1913 sabers were forged and became one of the cavalry's weapons.

In 1899, the Army developed land below Fort Whipple (now Whipple Field) and built several buildings, mainly to house the Signal Corps. Known as Lower Post, it stood separate from the upper post of Fort Myer. Though the 9th Cavalry had barracks and stables there, buildings were erected to accommodate the vision of the US Army's future in the skies. Observation balloons were used very successfully during the Civil War. The army called for a new way of conquering the air, and Fort Myer became the locus of the experiments that would mark the first lighter-than-air flights. The milestones in 1908 of the first flights of military aviation also included the first aviation fatality.

The 9th Cavalry arrived at Fort Myer on May 25, 1891, under the command of Maj. Guy Henry, who was a Medal of Honor recipient for his actions at Cold Harbor in 1864. Major Henry became the commander of Fort Myer. Henry Gate at Fort Myer is named after him. Troop K of the 9th Cavalry served at Fort Myer until October 3, 1894. (FMHO.)

MAJOR GUY V. HENRY
1891-94

After a successful arctic expedition, Maj. Gen. Adolphus W. Greely was appointed chief signal officer in 1887, a post he would hold for nearly 20 years. It was under his watch that telegraph lines were strung across the United States. He was also head of the Weather Service until 1891, when it was transferred to the US Agricultural Department. He was awarded the Medal of Honor at the age of 91. Along with several others, Greely founded the National Geographic Society in 1888. (NARA.)

The Signal Corps harnessed the signaling power of the sun. Heliograph drills allowed soldiers to use this system of signaling, which was comprised of a mirror catching the sun's rays—often seen in Hollywood Westerns. The best use of this technique was by the US Army in the southwest United States. (NARA.)

OFFICER'S QUARTERS.
ADMINISTRATION BUILDING IN REAR AND CENTRE

When the Signal Corps returned to Fort Myer, additional buildings were constructed, including these quarters for unmarried officers and an administration building on Lower Post just east of where Fort Whipple originally stood. (FMHO.)

The US Army Signal Corps still considered the high ground of Fort Myer ideal for practicing signal drills using wig-wag. One group of signalers would stand on what would become Whipple Field and others would stand at the base of the Washington Monument, and the two groups would practice sending messages to each other. (LOC.)

Command Headquarters was constructed in elaborate Victorian style with an appropriate complement of mortars and a healthy supply of cannonballs. The wood-frame buildings were later replaced by brick structures for safety reasons—as were all buildings on Fort Myer. (FMHO.)

To handle the misbehaved among the troops, a guardhouse was also built on post. Take note of the soldier on the left and the ones on the porch. They were predecessors of the military police, which would also be established and organized at Fort Myer's South Post in the 1940s. (FMHO.)

In this image is a comparison of semaphore (left) and wig-wag flags (right). Myer's signaling system should not be confused with semaphore signaling. The wig-wag system used a single flag; depending on the background and weather conditions, one of the two variations (white with a red square in center or red with a white square in center) was chosen and waved back and forth. It was a quasi-binary code conceptually similar to Morse Code. The semaphore system used two flags, and each character to be transmitted had a unique pattern for holding the flags. (NARA.)

With a huge population of horses supporting the cavalry and field artillery, Fort Myer required great amounts of feed and bedding material for the animals. Part of the soldiers' duties included storing the hay bales in the stable. (FMHO.)

The first riding arena was built in 1893 to provide the space and environment where both the cavalry and field artillery could drill and keep their skills sharp during the winter months or on days when the weather did not cooperate. It was consumed by fire and rebuilt; the cornerstone of the replacement was dated 1934. (FMHO.)

First built as housing for unmarried US Army officers, this structure was then named Wainwright Hall in honor of Gen. Jonathan Mayhew Wainwright, who commanded Fort Myer in the 1930s. In future years, it would continue to provide housing for those on temporary duty assignments—TDY. (FMHO.)

Quarters One, built in 1899, was originally the home of the commanding officer of Fort Myer. It has been the chief of staff of the Army's residence since 1908, when Maj. Gen. J. Franklin Bell occupied the home. When Gen. John J. "Black Jack" Pershing became chief of staff of the Army, he was one of the few who would not occupy this house on the high ground, opting to continue living in downtown Washington, DC. (NARA.)

Built in the 1890s, this became Fort Myer's Headquarters Building. It was later named for Gen. George S. Patton Jr. in recognition of his contributions to the US Army generally and Fort Myer specifically. The above was taken in the 1930s, when it had become the Officer's Club, and the lower photograph was taken in the 1960s, after the building was expanded to accommodate the growing need for an on-post gathering place. (Both FMHO.)

Hospital and Depot Fort Myer Va.

On the left of this photograph stands the post's hospital, and on the right is the trolley depot. In 1892, the Washington, Arlington, and Falls Church Railway was a horse-car line with tracks from Rosslyn up the hill to Fort Myer. A platform was attached to the passenger car, and the horse was unhitched, placed on the platform at the rear of the car, and allowed to coast down the hill on the return trip. In late 1895, the system was electrified. (LOC.)

The Officers' Equestrian Center was built near the entrance of Arlington National Cemetery. The trolley tracks of the Washington, Arlington, and Falls Church Railway are seen in the midground. The photograph was taken near where the Old Post Chapel would soon be erected. The equestrian center was used by the cavalry officers to keep their riding skills in top condition. In the background on the left are some of the stables, and to their right is the row of enlisted men's barracks. (FMHO.)

Two additional barracks were constructed in the early 1900s on Sheridan Avenue. One of them was building No. 249, which over time has had many lives. When the Great War was over, the first floor of the building became the headquarters of the 16th Field Artillery. (FMHO.)

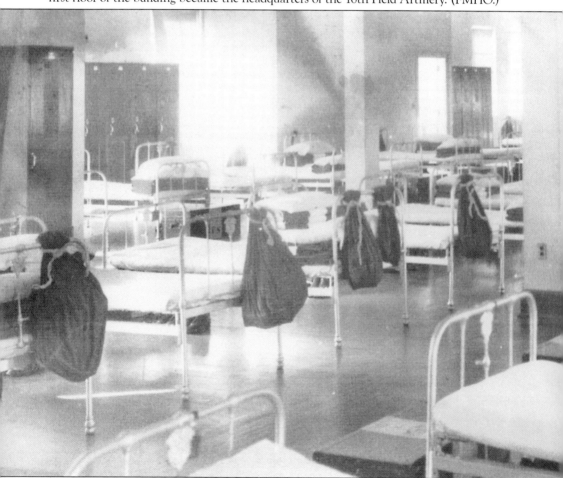

The unit's barracks had their living space on the upper floor. The photograph below shows the soldiers' bunks. The photograph at right shows the sergeant's bunk and locker ready for inspection. Later, the building would become the museum of the 3rd Infantry Regiment—the Old Guard—and showcase many of the regiment's artifacts, dating back to the Revolutionary War. (Both TOGM.)

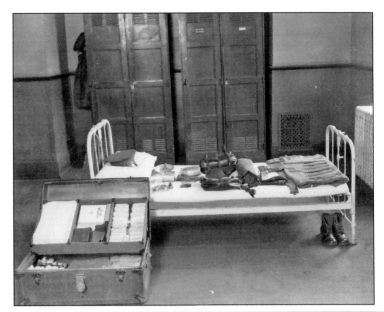

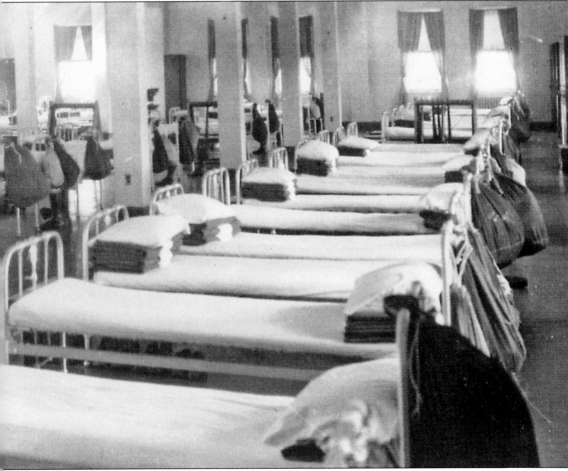

Another result of the aggressive expansion at Fort Myer is the Post Exchange—PX. Although it was the PX in April 1948, when the US Army's 3rd Infantry Regiment—the Old Guard—was reactivated and designated the ceremonial unit of the US Army, decades later, the building would become regimental headquarters. (LOC.)

This is Quarters Eight, which dates to 1903. It was part of the rebuilding and expansion that occurred from 1899 to 1915. Originally it was the Fort Myer post commander's quarters. When he was Fort Myer's commander and commander of the US Army's 3rd Cavalry, George S. Patton Jr. lived here from 1934 to 1938. (FMHO.)

It was only fitting that when the Signal Corps returned to Fort Myer in 1899 it would build a balloon barn on the Lower Post (below present-day Whipple Field). Observation balloons provided an aerial perspective that proved successful in the Civil War and complemented the weather service that originated in the Signal Corps on Fort Myer in 1870. (FMHO.)

A balloon was very limited in its movement and was subject to the whims of weather and wind. The US Army first considered a rigid airship—the dirigible—as an alternative. The airship was tested in 1908 and accepted by the US Army on August 28, 1908. Here, the first and only one that would be purchased is stored in the balloon barn on Fort Myer. (NARA.)

Equipped with engine power, the dirigible overcame some of the constraints of the weather. Here is the US Army's first one in flight. It allowed directed movement as well as all the observation benefits of being aloft. Unfortunately, because of its size, it was not easily maneuvered. (NARA.)

In 1908, the US Army tested this airship over Fort Myer's drill field with some degrees of success, but the ship was later abandoned because of its limited maneuverability and the development of more effective technologies. Lts. Frank Lahm, Thomas Selfridge, and Benjamin Foulois of the US Army Aeronautical Division were taught to fly it. (FMHO.)

As part of the US Army Aeronautical Division, Lts. Frank Lahm and Benjamin Foulois were pioneers in the US Army's pursuit of flight. They were the first to fly the dirigible that the Army tested and later abandoned. Lahm would become the first certified pilot in the US Army and retire as a brigadier general; Foulois would go on to be recognized as the US Army's first aviator and rise to major general. In July 1909, he was a passenger when Orville flew the 10 miles from Fort Myer to Alexandria City, Virginia, and back. He provided air service on General Pershing's punitive march into Mexico in pursuit of Pancho Villa. (LOC.)

Orville Wright (seen here) and his brother, Wilbur, were pioneers of flight. On September 01, 1908, the Wright Flyer arrived at Fort Myer, Virginia, aboard a wagon, attracting the attention of children and adults. Orville brought the Wright Flyer to Fort Myer to respond to the US Army's request for a heavier-than-air flying vehicle. (LOC.)

Lt Selfridge and Dr Alexandra Graham Bell--
Fort Myer, Virginia--1908

Here are two pioneers in the advancement of communications and aviation. On the right is Alexander Graham Bell, inventor of the telephone, and on the left is aviator Lt. Thomas Etholen Selfridge in civilian clothes. They were observing the tests of the Wright Flyer. Selfridge would also hold the sad distinction of becoming the first military aviation fatality as a result of the Wright Flyer crashing on September 17, 1908. (FMHO.)

Here is the Wright Flyer, which arrived on September 1, 1908. Testing did not begin until the 7th due to weather conditions. The Wright Flyer was stored in a barn on post before and during the testing period. (LOC.)

On September 7, testing began. Here the Wright Flyer is on Parade Field. In the near background is the expansive drill field of the post where the cavalry and field artillery honed their skills. It is framed by Arlington National Cemetery's wall in the background. (LOC.)

The Wright Flyer is prepared for takeoff. The flyer used a weighted-rope catapult to give it initial forward movement and lift. On the left is the post's hospital, where they would later take the injured Orville Wright and Lieutenant Selfridge. (FMHO.)

The Wright Flyer is aloft over the drill field during one of Orville's solo flights during the 10 days of testing. Lt. Frank Lahm would be the first to fly with Orville. Arlington National Cemetery's wall and the gate that would be named for Lieutenant Selfridge are seen in the background. (FMHO.)

Despite the crash on September 17, 1908, it was determined that the Wright brothers had a viable answer and were invited back to Fort Myer in July 1909 for further testing and final acceptance of the Wright Flyer. Here, aviation pioneers Lt. Frank Lahm and Glenn Hammond Curtiss, designer and test pilot of the "June Bug," an early US aircraft, observe the 1909 trials of the Wright Flyer on Fort Myer—among the flights were a long-distance one in which Lt. Benjamin Foulois flew with Orville. (LOC.)

Here is the corral of 15th Cavalry in the early 1900s showing some of the horses on Fort Myer. At one point, there were nearly 1,500 horses on the post in support of the cavalry and field artillery units stationed there. The mounts required a continual and consistent amount of care and attention. (LOC.)

The precision tactical moves by the cavalry required consistent and repeated drills. This is a regimental formation of 15th Cavalry on the drill field waiting to be inspected by the post's commander. (LOC.)

The riding arena provided an environment for the troopers to conduct their tactical drills in inclement weather. Here is the 15th Cavalry preparing to enter the hall. Notice the protective head gear worn by the troopers in the center between the two troopers with guidons. (LOC.)

The troopers would become one with their horses. Not only would the soldiers acquire great skills, they would also spend time training their horses to do tricks such as this "Sit down, and take a load off your feet" display. (LOC.)

When tactical training was complete, troopers would engage in competitions and stunts and practice daredevil formations. Although stationary for this photograph, they would often be seen racing down the drill field in a display of showmanship and daring. (LOC.)

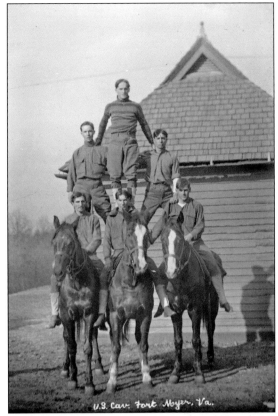

U.S. Cav. Fort Myer, Va.

Some of the stunts and feats of wonder went a bit overboard, adding amusement to the awe factor of the horse show. Here soldiers are supposedly having a meal, only to be interrupted by one of their fellow troopers, who jumps his horse over their dining table. (LOC.)

The cadets of Virginia Military Institute (VMI) would spend part of their summers at Fort Myer attending summer camp. A cadet bugler would provide the cadets their notices with bugle calls. Several post commanders were VMI graduates, including Col. Harry Cootes. (LOC.)

At one time, each regiment had its own band—a source of entertainment and a morale booster for the soldiers. This is the 15th US Cavalry Band on North Parade Field, which would draw upon its history and heritage and eventually be renamed Whipple Field. (LOC.)

Band 15th Cav. U.S. army.

When the regiment went on field maneuvers, the 15th Cavalry's band went with it. Fort Meade, Maryland, was probably where this photograph was taken, since it had ranges and open spaces to conduct live-fire drills on post. Fort Myer lacked that space then and still does. (LOC.)

The US Army—especially the cavalry units—responded and moved to bugle calls. Drums were also used when available to signal and call the troops to desired action. Here are the 15th Cavalry buglers on field maneuvers. (LOC.)

Today, very little is known about US Army remount depots that were constructed to provide the forces with an ongoing supply of fine horses and mules. The postcard highlights the US Army Remount Depot at Front Royal, Virginia—Kidron and Jeff were Gen. John J. "Black Jack" Pershing's horses. The US government purchased 5,000 acres south of Front Royal in the early 1900s for a remount depot. Horses were brought into town to the train station and driven to the remount depot along Route 522. The horses were vaccinated, trained, and quarantined before being sent to US cavalry units. General Pershing's horses are buried on the property. (FMHO.)

Thousands of horses were collected and prepared for distribution to the cavalry and field artillery units within the US Army. During World War I, the needs were great and the action ongoing, as shown in this remount depot at Camp Kearny near San Diego, California. The impact of the

The US Army acquired its horses from surrounding farms that were designated as the breeding farms according to the specifications provided. The remount depot functioned as a collection point for these animals and provided acreage where the horses could be vaccinated, trained, and exercised. During World War II, the Front Royal, Virginia, Remount Depot was the site for training mules used to carry cargoes of military supplies over terrain not suited for motorized vehicles in the European and China-Burma-India theaters. The remount depot became the home for all of the Lipizzaner studs that were removed from Europe under the direction of Gen. George S. Patton Jr. Today the Smithsonian Institute operates a conservation center on part of the property for the study of endangered species. There is also a training facility for drug-sniffing dogs as well as the Northern Virginia 4-H Center. (NARA.)

US Army's Remount Service has had far reaching effects up until today because of the military's rigid requirements for the horses; unprecedented standards were set for many of today's horses across multiple breed lines. (LOC.)

In the 1916 image above, a final honors procession is escorted by the 15th Cavalry. Capt. Charles T. Boyd, 10th Cavalry, US Army, had been killed in action at the Battle of Carrizal during the Punitive Expedition, and here, his funeral procession is shown as it crosses the Aqueduct Bridge from Georgetown to Rosslyn, Virginia, in what was then still Alexandria County, and then on to Arlington National Cemetery. Not until 1933 would the Memorial Bridge near the Lincoln Memorial be built, figuratively and literally connecting the North and the South. In the image below, the 15th Cavalry Final Honors Procession Escort continues on to Arlington National Cemetery to provide military honors to the fallen veteran. (Both LOC.)

In this 1914 photograph, a squad of soldiers marches up the road in front of the Enlisted Solders Barracks. Two of the buildings were constructed in 1894, and additional ones would follow to meet the growing needs of Fort Myer. The dirt road would soon give way to asphalt with sidewalks and curbs. The building on the right is the PX and would eventually become headquarters for the Old Guard. (LOC.)

Far from General Sheridan's vision of showcasing the cavalry, Fort Myer became the showcase for the US Army, and many ceremonies and events have been held on post over time. It was often visited by presidents, statesmen, and domestic and foreign dignitaries attending various events. Visiting in 1913, Pres. Woodrow Wilson and Secretary of War Lindley Miller Garrison make their way to a ceremony on the South Parade Field. (LOC.)

Maj. Charles Pelot Summerall was commander of Fort Myer in 1913 while the 3rd Field Artillery was stationed on post. An 1892 graduate of West Point, he would return there to be the senior artillery instructor. Serving in World War I, he would be promoted to major general. He would ultimately be promoted to general and serve as chief of staff of the US Army from 1926 to 1930. Fort Myer's South Parade Field is named in his honor. (FMHO.)

MAJOR CHARLES P. SUMMERALL 1913

Rodney was a retired horse at Fort Myer. Rodney would later be recognized first by an artilleryman, Leonard Hastings Nason (1895–1970), a journalist and author specializing in stories recounting his experiences in World War I. His short story, "Rodney," appeared in the January 21, 1933, edition of the *Saturday Evening Post*. Later that year, Hollywood came to Fort Myer to film the 1934 movie *Keep 'em Rolling*, based on Nason's story. Although already popular with the Army, the movie also introduced a musical number to the public, "The Caissons Go Rolling Along," written by Lt. Edmund L. Gruber. Once the lyrics were changed, it would come to be known officially as "The Army Song." (LOC.)

As World War I continued to spread in Europe, the United States prepared for the inevitable, and Fort Myer became one of the posts where reserve officer training was conducted. The South Parade Field became the central location for the candidates' physical training—PT. (LOC.)

Among the buildings constructed for the Reserve Officer Training Corps was the officers' own mess hall. Here is the interior showing them enjoying a meal. This one particular building would remain long after their training ended to serve the needs of the other soldiers stationed at Fort Myer. (LOC.)

Summerall Field, also known as the South Parade Field, was where the ROTC barracks and mess hall "tempos"—temporary buildings—were built. Surrounding the closest one is a line of ROTC trainees who appear to be going for a meal. In the distance are the radio transmission towers known as the "Three Sisters," not to be confused with the rock formation in the Potomac River. (LOC.)

With the training completed, the ROTC class of 1917 poses for a group portrait on the north end of the South Parade Field. In the background on the left are the officers' quarters, which face Lee

Automobiles fill the foreground of this image as members of the ROTC class of 1917 attend their commencement ceremonies on the South Parade Field. Arrayed along the background from left to right are the original riding arena, the PX, and the buildings on Jackson Avenue. (LOC.)

Avenue. On the right are the class's barracks. (LOC.)

The first wireless communication towers, these three radio towers, known as the "Three Sisters" and similar to the Eiffel Tower in construction, were erected in 1913 at the southwest end of Fort Myer. One stood 600 feet high, and the other two stood 450 feet above the 200-foot elevation of the site. The word "radio" was first used (instead of "wireless") in the name of this naval communications facility. The first transatlantic voice communication was made between this station and the Eiffel Tower in 1915. The nation set its clocks by the signal and listened for its broadcast weather reports. The towers were dismantled in 1941 as a menace to aircraft approaching the new Washington National Airport. They were relocated to Annapolis, Maryland. (LOC.)

Here are the boxers of Fort Myer. Many different athletic programs were arranged and provided for the soldiers within the US Army. Gen. George S. Patton Jr. introduced football within the US Army to keep the soldiers from drinking and gambling. Several of those teams lasted until the mid-1960s, many posts fielding a team. Fort Myer did not field a football team, unlike Fort Benning, Georgia. Fort Benning's Doughboys football team was once coached by Dwight D. Eisenhower, called the "Kansas Cyclone" when he was posted there. He later ended up as a five-star general and chief of staff of the US Army and lived at Fort Myer in Quarters One. (FMHO.)

By the 1900s, all the wood-frame buildings had been replaced. These are the quarters on Jackson Avenue's "Officers' Row," which faced the North Parade Field (later called Whipple Field) and offered a view of the city of Washington, DC. (LOC.)

Unlike what is normally the design, where the front of the quarters faces the parade field, the quarters on Officers' Row on Lee Avenue faced the street, and to their backs was the South Parade Field, which would later be called Summerall Field in honor of Gen. William Pelot Summerall, US Army chief of staff. (LOC.)

Whether by horse or by automobile, General Pershing was ready to ride. The nickname "Black Jack" came about from his commanding of the Buffalo Soldiers at San Juan Hill in Cuba in 1898 during the Spanish-American War. Pershing would become chief of staff of the US Army in 1921 but chose not to live in Quarters One on Fort Myer, instead continuing to live in Washington, DC. (LOC.)

The mechanization of the US Army began slowly. Leaders were provided with staff cars as conveniences, such as General Pershing's car, seen here. However, notice the spurs on his boots in the photograph at left: it would be years before the US Army would fully leave horses behind. (LOC.)

Four

BETWEEN THE WARS

After World War I, the US Army's 3rd Cavalry—known as the "Brave Rifles," a name given to them by Gen. Winfield Scott—returned to Fort Myer. The 16th Field Artillery shared the post with them as Lt. Col. William O. Reed of 3rd Cavalry became post commander. The next two decades would be filled with many notable milestones. In 1846, when a parcel of land that was contributed to form the District of Columbia was returned to the Commonwealth of Virginia, the land surrounding Fort Myer became known as Alexandria County. It was formally renamed Arlington County in 1920.

During the 1920s and 1930s, the regiment underwent a series of organizational changes. Second Squadron, plus C and D Troops of 1st Squadron, were deactivated. Third Squadron was redesignated as 2nd Squadron and stationed at Fort Myer, Virginia. This unit was becoming known as the "President's Own." With its proximity to Washington and Arlington National Cemetery, the 2nd Squadron was frequently called upon to furnish honor guards and escorts for distinguished visitors and funeral escorts for important civilian officials and military personnel.

On November 11, 1921, the regiment furnished the cavalry escort for the burial of the Unknown Soldier from World War I in Arlington National Cemetery. Until 1941, the regiment provided the guard detail at the Tomb of the Unknown Soldier. By the time Col. George S. Patton Jr. returned for the fourth time and became commander of Fort Myer in 1938, many milestone events had been recorded, including the building of the Old Post Chapel, dedicated in April 1935. Fort Myer became the location of the Society Circus, which would present the talents of the soldiers to residents within the Washington, DC, area—shows of equestrian skills combined with pageantry that would continue the showcase vision begun by Gen. Philip H. Sheridan.

Here Gen. John J. Pershing is mounted on Kidron on the east side of the drill field as he reviews the troops. Among the trees behind him is Arlington National Cemetery's west wall. On the left side in the background are some of the training stations for the cavalry. (LOC.)

The 3rd Cavalry Band on the South Parade Field (known as Summerall Field) may be waiting for the adjutant's call to begin a parade or review of the troops. On the left behind them are the two pylons marking the goal for polo matches. In the near background are the enlisted men's barracks seen through the trees on Sheridan Avenue. (NARA.)

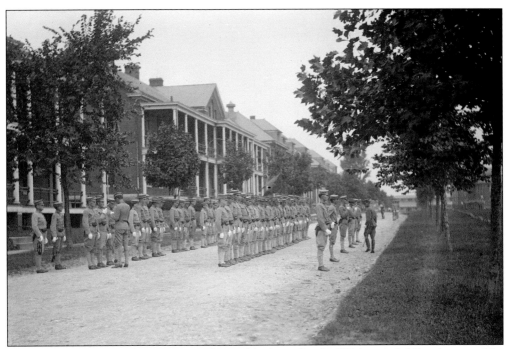

On a still-unpaved Sheridan Avenue, in front of the barracks, the US Army's 3rd Cavalry assembles in an inspection formation. Given that most of the men are wearing white gloves, this is a "white glove inspection," which kept the soldiers to high standards required by the US Army. Any bit of dirt or grease on their weapons would show up on the gloves. (LOC.)

This is another squad of the US Army's 3rd Cavalry assembled for inspection before its next mission. (LOC.)

For nearly two decades, final honors support within Arlington National Cemetery was provided by the 3rd Cavalry. Here the three-volley salute is executed by what might have been the entire marching escort at Maj. Gen. William Crawford Gorgas's final honors in 1920. He was surgeon general of the US Army from 1914 until his retirement in 1918. Gorgas's success in reducing the infections of yellow fever made the Panama Canal possible. (NARA.)

During the winter months or inclement weather, the 16th Field Artillery Battery would go indoors to conduct drill practice in the riding arena. Split-second timing is a key factor when they are firing the traditional 21-gun salute for the president or the round-specific salutes (11, 13, 15, or 17) for flag officers' honors. (LOC.)

The soldiers assigned to Fort Myer had more than ceremonial duties and responsibilities. To keep its tactical skills honed, the 3rd Cavalry set up on the Fort Myer drill field and conducted Field Camp with its tents arrayed in bivouac style. (LOC.)

Over time, additional acreage on Fort Myer was acquired to ease the training needs of the 3rd Cavalry soldiers. Several trails were constructed with "enemy targets" along them for saber practice. (NARA.)

In the earlier days, the reviewing stand was constructed and set on the east side of the South Parade Field (later named Summerall Field), providing ample seating for the attendees of the horse shows, changes of commands, parades, and other events that would be held there. (FMHO.)

The horse shows featured other displays of skill. Performing maneuvers that went far beyond the *Manual of Arms*, the 3rd Cavalry would include a demonstration of a rifle drill. These displays are thought by some to have been the beginnings of the US Army Drill Team that would follow when the 3rd US Infantry, "the Old Guard," was ultimately reactivated and stationed at Fort Myer. (NARA.)

Troopers were encouraged to be creative in showcasing their equestrian skills. Each squadron developed specialties to impress the attendees. Here, the US Army's 3rd Cavalry has a friendly little competition during one of the horse shows. (FMHO.)

To add variety to the horse show skills demonstration, the troopers of the US Army's 3rd Cavalry might conduct a pushball competition mounted on their horses. (LOC.)

The horse shows provided feats of daring and skill. Here, another set of troopers from the 3rd Cavalry presents a "Roman-style" riding demonstration. (LOC.)

Often the US Army's cavalry would train to compete and represent the United States in the Olympics, and jumping hurdles might be parts of the competition. It also made a good display of coordination and skills that the troopers developed. (NARA.)

Sgt. Frank Witchey of the 3rd Cavalry Regiment sounded Taps at the interment of the Unknown Soldier on November 11, 1921, with President Harding presiding. Witchey also sounded Taps for the funerals of Pres. Woodrow Wilson, Lt. Gen. Nelson A. Miles, Lt. Gen. S.B.M. Young, Maj. Gen. Leonard Wood, and Col. William Jennings Bryan. The bugle used by Sergeant Witchey was the one originally issued to him by the Army. The day after he sounded Taps for the Unknown Soldier on Armistice Day 1921, he bought it from the quartermaster for $2.50. He had the instrument gold-plated, and a record of all the important ceremonies at which it was sounded was engraved on it. He retired in 1938 after 30 years of service. (FMHO.)

In 1926, William John Quick, of the 3rd Cavalry Headquarters Troop posted at Fort Myer, was one of the first sentinels—the honor guard at the Tomb of the Unknown Soldier within Arlington National Cemetery. Until March 1926, the tomb had a civilian guard. (FMHO.)

Pfc. John W. McCoy, a 3rd Cavalry trooper, is an honor guard at the Tomb of the Unknown Soldier, continuing the guarding of this sacred place within Arlington National Cemetery. Upon reactivation of the 3rd Infantry Regiment in 1948, soldiers from the regiment would be selected as sentinels. (FMHO.)

Col. Guy V. Henry Jr. was an 1898 graduate of West Point, where he was director of the cavalry school from 1916 to 1918. He fought in the Spanish-American War, the Philippine Insurrection, World War I, and World War II. Colonel Henry was later awarded the Silver Star. He represented the United States in the 1912 Olympics, earning a bronze medal. When he became commander of Fort Myer from 1927 to 1930, he was the second Guy V. Henry to do so. (FMHO.)

Col. Guy V. Henry Jr., commander of Fort Myer and the 3rd Cavalry, accompanies Secretary of War James W. Good as they inspect a formation of troopers. The building directly behind the line of soldiers is the post's theater, which was still under construction. To its left is the PX. (LOC.)

Polo was one of the sports that tested the skills of the soldiers, and nearly every US Army post fielded a team. Here are two images of a polo match on Fort Myer's South Parade Field (later Summerall Field). Individuals or entire teams would be selected to travel to other US Army posts to compete against local polo clubs. (Both LOC.)

Gen. Charles Pelot Summerall (center forward) and Col. Guy V. Henry Jr. (to his right) review the troops of the Citizens Military Training Camps. Authorized by the US National Defense Act of 1920, the CMTC provided young volunteers with four weeks of military training in summer camps each year from 1921 to 1941. Approximately 30,000 trainees participated each year. Those who voluntarily completed four summers of CMTC training became eligible for reserve commissions. At the end of the camp, individuals were presented with awards for their achievements during the session. (Both LOC.)

Down the street from the Post Exchange (PX) and across from the riding arena on Sheridan Avenue is the Fort Myer Theater, where movies were shown and other events were held to provide on-post entertainment for the soldiers. (FMHO.)

This was the post library, which provided both information and entertainment for the soldiers. It was located on Sheridan Avenue next to the Post Theater near the South Parade Field (later known as Summerall Field) and across from the enlisted men's barracks. (FMHO.)

Gen. Douglas MacArthur served as chief of staff of the US Army from 1930 to 1935 and occupied Quarters One during that time. One of the five-star generals—general of the Army—MacArthur's earlier career included commandant at West Point and receiving the Distinguished Service Cross in World War I for his service there as part of the American Expeditionary Force. In 1932, when the Bonus Expeditionary Force began to clash in Washington, MacArthur was ordered by President Hoover to "surround the affected area and clear it without delay" with soldiers from Fort Myer and other nearby installations. General of the Army MacArthur was later awarded the Medal of Honor just like his father, Arthur MacArthur Jr., and they thus became the first father and son to be awarded this highest military honor. (LOC.)

COLONEL HARRY N. COOTES
1930-33

Harry Newton Cootes became the commander of both the 3rd Cavalry Regiment and Fort Myer from 1930 to 1933. He first attended Staunton Military Academy, and then he moved on to the Virginia Military Institute, where he graduated. During his command, the Machine Gun Troop of the 10th Cavalry arrived at Fort Myer in 1931. They and their horses would occupy buildings on Lower Post, the area below Whipple Field, and stay until 1949. (FMHO.)

(0769-840M·BF)(3-20-30-10:32 A)(12-1000)

In an aerial photograph facing northwest, the "Three Sisters" radio towers are seen in the lower left corner. Fort Myer occupies the upper right corner, with the wall of Arlington National Cemetery marking the eastern boundary. The light area within that corner is the drill field, and below is the maze of trails used for tactical training. Gun sheds and stables of the field artillery are on the left. (NARA.)

767-840M·BF)(3-20-30-10:30A)(12-900)
RADIO TOWERS ARLINGTON, VA.

This east-facing 1930 aerial photograph shows the immensity of the "Three Sisters" in the foreground. In the background across the entire photograph is Arlington National Cemetery. Above that is Arlington Farms. In less than a decade, the War Department would erect the Pentagon in the right corner of that space, while turning part of it into the Arlington Cantonment, which would later become Fort Myer's South Post. (NARA.)

With their "Patton Swords" (designated as the M1913) drawn, the 10th Cavalry, Machine Gun Troop K, are mounted on their horses in regimental formation on South Parade Field (later known as Summerall Field) at Fort Myer. The enlisted men's barracks are across the background. One of the tempos, used as a mess hall, stands in front of the barracks. (NARA.)

In 1932, Secretary of State Henry Lewis Stimson and Col. Harry Newton Cootes, commander of Fort Myer, inspect and review the Machine Gun Troop of the US Army's 10th Cavalry Regiment (Buffalo Soldiers) at Fort Myer. The troopers have their distinctive buffalo guidons on their lances. Stimson had also served as secretary of war and would do so again after his service as secretary of state. (NARA.)

Holding true as a showplace for horse-mounted troops, in 1931, Fort Myer claimed the distinction of having the first and only Mounted Cub Scout Pack. The image above shows the Mounted Cub Scout Pack; below is the pack's color guard. These photographs were donated to the Fort Myer History Office's archives by George Allin. Colonel Allin was one of these mounted Cub Scouts. (Both FMHO.)

In the photograph at left is the unveiling of the memorial to Brig. Gen. Albert J. Myer in 1932. The photograph below shows part of the group in attendance: Seen here from left to right are Col. Harry Newton Cootes, cavalry; Maj. Gen. George O. Squier; USA (Ret.); Gertrude W. Myer (daughter of General Myer); Brig. Gen. George P. Scriven, USA (Ret.); Maj. Gen. Irving J. Carr, chief signal officer of the Army; and Col. Campbell B. Hodges, infantry, military aide to the president of the United States. The memorial is located on Whipple Field. (Both NARA.)

The Bonus Expedition Force came to Washington, DC. Few images from the Great Depression are more indelible than the rout of the Bonus Marchers. On the steamy morning of July 28, 1932, several marchers rushed Chief of Police Major Glassford's officers and began throwing bricks. President Hoover ordered the secretary of war to "surround the affected area and clear it without delay." (NARA)

Commanded by Douglas MacArthur, US Army troops (including Maj. George S. Patton Jr. who commanded six tanks, and Maj. Dwight D. Eisenhower, who acted as General MacArthur's aide) formed infantry cordons and began pushing the veterans out, destroying their makeshift camps as they went. Although no weapons were fired, cavalry advanced with swords drawn, and some blood was shed. By nightfall, hundreds had been injured by gas, bricks, clubs, bayonets, and sabers. One baby died. (NARA.)

A fire destroyed the first Fort Myer Riding Arena, which was built in 1893. From the ashes, a new arena arose that was ready for use in 1934, providing a place for the cavalry and field artillery soldiers to continue to hone their skills and deliver demonstrations of their horsemanship. (FMHO.)

The interior of the new Fort Myer Riding Arena provided facilities for the cavalry and field artillery to exercise and hone their equestrian skills. By the late 1940s, as the US Army became mechanized and gave up its horses, the riding arena would no longer have the pounding hooves nor the dirt floor. It is now named Conmy Hall for Joseph B. Conmy Jr., a heavily decorated Army infantry colonel who received the coveted Combat Infantryman Badge in three wars and commanded the US Army's 3rd Infantry Regiment. (NARA.)

With Fort Myer's horse population at nearly 1,500, there was need for a small army of farriers to replace the shoes of the mounts of the post's cavalry and field artillery. Shoeing and reshoeing the mounts kept them busy. (FMHO.)

In 1934, a new Enlisted Men's Quarters, known as Building 251, was added along Sheridan Avenue to accommodate the growth of the soldier population on Fort Myer. By this time, the road was paved, and sidewalks and curbs were in place. (FMHO.)

When George S. Patton Jr. arrived for his third tour of duty at Fort Myer, the latest addition to the installation was the new post chapel, which was dedicated on Easter Sunday in 1935. Since then, the chapel has been the site of many weddings. Many of the final honors ceremonies begin in this beautiful structure. The stained-glass windows, installed later, are memorable: each one is dedicated to a branch of military service. (FMHO.)

COLONEL JONATHAN WAINWRIGHT
1936–38

When promoted to colonel in 1936, Jonathan Wainwright had his second tour on Fort Myer. This time, he was commander of the 3rd Cavalry and Fort Myer. He left Fort Myer as a brigadier general and went to the Philippines before World War II. When Gen. Douglas MacArthur went to Australia in 1942, Wainwright was promoted to lieutenant general in charge of all US Army forces in the Philippines. For his actions in the Pacific, he would earn the Medal of Honor. (FMHO.)

The building expansion would continue on post. On the south end of Fort Myer, workers of the Works Projects Administration (WPA) built new stables and gun sheds for field artillery. First used to house World War I French 75 millimeter artillery, the gun sheds for field artillery would in time be used by the Presidential Salute Battery of the Old Guard—the 3rd Infantry Regiment of the US Army. (Both FMHO.)

On the north end of Fort Myer, WPA workers built new stables and a new administration building for the cavalry. Below, the new building for the cavalry would ultimately become the tack building, where the harnesses and other items of tack for the horses are still made by hand. (Both FMHO.)

In addition to providing final honors support in Arlington National Cemetery, the soldiers at Fort Myer also participate in parades, inaugurals, and more. In the above image is the 16th Field Artillery on parade in downtown Washington, DC; below is the 3rd Cavalry, also participating in that same parade. These two photographs of FDR's 1937 inauguration were donated by Capt. Robert McAfee of Arlington County, Virginia. (Both FMHO.)

The Society Circus, which began after World War I, continued until World War II. Dressed in show or stage uniform, the 16th Field Artillery poses here in front of its barracks along Sheridan Avenue, ready for its role in the review. The barracks, Building 249, later became home to the Old Guard Museum and Headquarters to the US Army's 3rd Infantry Regiment. (LOC.)

Drawing upon their experiences in the American West, the soldiers used their creativity to provide the socialites of Washington, DC, with a glimpse of a part of the United States that many may have never seen—cavalry soldiers by day, by night they were singing cowboys for the Society Circus within the riding arena. (FMHO.)

George Patton, during his second tour on Fort Myer, had first proposed the Society Circus—and what is a circus without clowns? The creative side of the soldiers is reflected in some of the troops' costumes. (LOC.)

Even the band got involved with what look like elaborate clown costumes, which probably delighted the audiences. Their performance was complemented by a number of equestrian acts of daring and skill. (LOC.)

Another duty of a cavalry or field artillery soldier was responsibility for his horse. Part of that duty included the grooming of his mount. He kept his horse's mane and all other parts of his horse trimmed close to present a uniform appearance. Here, one soldier holds the reins of the horse while the other uses the clippers. (NARA.)

Sen. Morris Sheppard of Texas, chairman of the Senate Military Affairs Committee, inspects the Machine Gun Unit of the 3rd Cavalry, US Army, at Fort Myer, Virginia. He is shown with Col. Jonathan Mayhew Wainwright, commander at Fort Myer. Colonel Wainwright is wearing an officer's cape. The dark blue cape with branch color lining was a normal item of military dress uniform worn often in that formal era. (LOC.)

Col. Jonathan M. Wainwright, commanding officer of Fort Myer, was promoted to the rank of brigadier general. The highest ranking non-commissioned officers of the post, Sgt. Maj. Timothy Carragher of the 16th Field Artillery (left) and Sgt. Maj. Frank Benegas of the 3rd Cavalry, were chosen to pin the stars on the new general's shoulders. By this time, Brigadier General Wainwright had commanded the 3rd Cavalry for more than two years. (LOC.)

Col. George S. Patton Jr. commanded the 3rd Cavalry and was Fort Myer's commander from 1938 to 1940. Over his career, Patton was stationed at Fort Myer four times. The first was when he was attached to the 15th Cavalry and designed the "Patton Sword." His contributions continued, such as establishing the first football team within the US Army and the 1st Armored Division. From here, he went on to become a lieutenant general and commanded the Third Army in World War II. After the war, he was promoted to full general, entitled to wearing four stars. (FMHO.)

The above image shows the commissary and bakery built on Lower Post below Whipple Field to provide a resource for the soldiers and their families. In the lower image, the interior of the commissary is shown as a captain walks by neat well-stocked shelves with his wife. (Both FMHO.)

Colonel Patton established the Society Circus during his second tour at Fort Myer to both raise money for the Soldiers' Relief Fund and to keep the members of the 3rd Cavalry sharp in their equestrian skills. It also allowed the soldiers to display other skills and talents. (FMHO.)

Part of the Society Circus included a display of the pageantry of the US Army. Here, the 3rd Cavalry presents its colors—the US flag, regimental flag, and troop guidons. This would later evolve into the US Army's Spirit of America, which is held at various locations across the United States. (FMHO.)

Everyone got involved in the celebration and production of this annual event. Here wives, girlfriends, and others related to the troopers of the 3rd Cavalry E Troop leave the riding arena after their riding and revue in the Society Circus. (LOC.)

The daughter of Col. George S. Patton Jr., Beatrice Patton, is shown here after participating in the Society Circus. It has been said that she had her father's temperament and riding skills. (LOC.)

Fort Myer was often the choice of where to test new developments in US Army, so in 1938, when the Army chose to change its uniforms, these soldiers dressed in the new uniforms that became standard across the entire army. Pictured are officers in mounted and dismounted uniforms. (NARA.)

For his fourth and final tour at Fort Myer, Col. George S. Patton became post commander and commanded the US Army's 3rd Cavalry. He is seen here on the drill field reviewing the troops. In the background, with the dust rising, outlines of the Three Sisters can be seen. (FMHO.)

As the world prepared for war, the US Army continued to rely upon its cavalry troopers and horses. A special truck was designed to move the men, the tack, and their horses in a very comfortable way. Mechanization of the Army was quickly approaching, a new way of fighting that would dramatically change the landscape of warfare. (Both FMHO.)

When the US Army moved by horse, limber and caisson wagons were standard means to move things. Origins date back to the early 19th century, and their use in traditions has continued long after the Army became mechanized. Final honors at Arlington National Cemetery continue to use the limber and caisson; a dedicated platoon of Fort Myer soldiers is trained using the *1942 Field Artillery Manual*. (NARA.)

The US Army also considered amphibious vehicles to move the troops quickly both on land and through the water. Fort Myer had its land, and a short drive down to the Potomac River permitted the Army to test the vehicle's performance in the water as members of the US Department of War observed. (NARA.)

Gen. George Catlett Marshall was promoted from brigadier to four-star general and became the 15th chief of staff of the Army on September 1, 1939, the same day that Hitler invaded Poland to start World War II. He would move into Fort Myer's Quarters One in August. Marshall would grow the size of the US Army 40-fold in three years. It was a time when the Army controlled not only the land but also the air with the Army Air Forces. (LOC.)

The 16th Field Artillery, Battery "C" is firing a 21-gun salute for Pres. Franklin D. Roosevelt upon his arrival at Arlington National Cemetery. The battery is located along what was the roadbed of the East Arlington branch of the Washington, Alexandria, and Mount Vernon Railway in the northeast part of the Custis-Lee estate. Their horses are seen at the end of the road. The Sheridan gate of the cemetery is on the far right. (FMHO.)

Five

WORLD WAR II

After Hitler invaded Poland in September 1939, war raged in Europe as the Nazi empire pushed to the east and occupied North Africa. It was not much better in Asia, as Japan flexed its might and also pushed west but ultimately east. Their attack on Pearl Harbor drew the United States into the war.

The US War Department was already planning for such a likelihood and was making preparations. Gen. George C. Marshall remained the chief of staff of the US Army during World War II. The landscape in and around what once was Arlington Farms, the flatlands near the Potomac River that was part of the 1,100 acres of the Custis-Lee estate, would change significantly.

Soon the Pentagon would be built in record time, and it was the largest office building in the world at the time. From the acreage would first emerge Arlington Cantonment. Eventually most of it would become South Post of Fort Myer. The land was in use by the US Department of Agriculture to grow experimental crops. Then came the War Department's requisition of the land to provide housing for those soldiers who would work in the newly constructed Pentagon.

Additionally, by the end of World War II, nearly 2,000 WACs would be housed within the confines of South Post. Then Headquarters Company, which was comprised of soldiers who also worked in the Pentagon and was organized and constituted in 1955, was housed here. By the late 1960s, the need for more space within Arlington National Cemetery became apparent and the need for South Post of Fort Myer to exist ceased, and by 1975, all the post's buildings were razed. Headquarters Company would find a new home on North Post of Fort Myer, where it is still headquartered today.

Soldiers of Battery A of the 16th Field Artillery are dressed in American Revolutionary–period uniforms with an appropriate period artillery piece. The equestrian area where many officers trained for the Olympics is behind them. Part of the hospital building on Lee Avenue can be seen in the upper left, while the upper right shows that additional officer housing has been built on the right side of the street. (FMHO.)

Battery A of the 16th Field Artillery, dressed in American Revolution uniforms, fire their cannon during the horse show in the riding arena on Fort Myer. As World War II's intensity rose, this would be the last of the Society Circus performances. Soon, the soldiers would be heading "over there" again. (FMHO.)

American Bantam Car Company was one of two that responded to the US Army's request for a four-wheel-drive reconnaissance car. Designed in two days, it was built in Butler, Pennsylvania, from off-the-shelf parts and tested on Fort Myer. In the center background of the upper image are the bases of the "Three Sisters"—those towers would not remain very long. In the lower image, the terrain of Fort Myer allowed for significant testing to occur, and the US Army adopted the vehicle for use in World War II. Nearly 640,000 Jeeps were produced during the war. (Both LOC.)

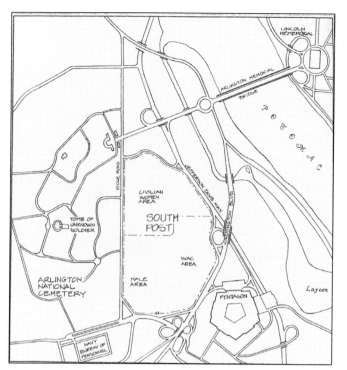

These two maps best show Fort Myer's South Post, which was part of Arlington Farms that the War Department requisitioned as part of war mobilization after the decision was made on the location of the Pentagon. The land was slowly relinquished. The southern portion became Arlington Cantonment. The northern section had housing built for the women who would be working within Washington, DC, during World War II. Arlington Cantonment would become South Post of Fort Myer and provide housing and more for nearly 2,000 WACs and soldiers who would work in the newly constructed Pentagon. (Both ICW.)

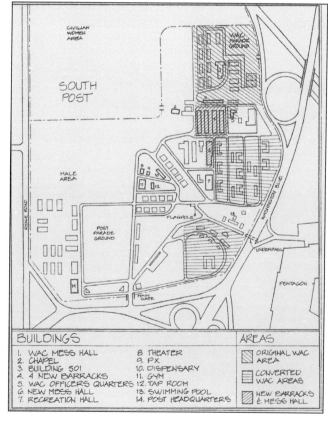

BUILDINGS		AREAS
1. WAC MESS HALL	8. THEATER	ORIGINAL WAC AREA
2. CHAPEL	9. PX	
3. BUILDING 501	10. DISPENSARY	CONVERTED WAC AREAS
4. 4 NEW BARRACKS	11. GYM	
5. WAC OFFICERS QUARTERS	12. TAP ROOM	NEW BARRACKS & MESS HALL
6. NEW MESS HALL	13. SWIMMING POOL	
7. RECREATION HALL	14. POST HEADQUARTERS	

The sign in the photograph above proudly proclaims "Arlington Farms." It would be the last reminder of what had been farming area since the Custis-Lee estate was established. The US Department of Agriculture had used the acreage for years to grow experimental crops. The photograph to the left shows the erected buildings that became housing for the women working in the Washington, DC, area during World War II. Afterwards, Arlington National Cemetery would have other plans for the area, including a visitor center, administration building, and gravesites. (Both LOC.)

On these two pages are aerial photographs taken in the 1960s. In this one, looking east, South Post of Fort Myer is in the foreground, with the post's Headquarters Building in the center. Additional buildings included a chapel, a movie theater, dining facilities (mess hall), and a gymnasium. Barracks for those working in the Pentagon, soldiers in Headquarters Company, are to the right. The cars in the center background belonged to people who drove to work at the Pentagon. (NARA.)

This aerial photograph was taken from behind the South Post of Fort Myer's Headquarters Building looking west. The barracks are clearly in the center of the photograph, with Arlington National Cemetery running across the entire background. After the war and through the 1960s or early 1970s, they provided housing for Headquarters Company. By 1975, the buildings were razed. All of this land would become cemetery. (NARA.)

The upper image was captured at the War College. The US Army Band—"Pershing's Own"—became a reality from an American Expeditionary Force band formed in France in 1918. It originally called Fort Hunt, Virginia, home when it was formally organized in 1922. It moved to the War College in Washington, DC—which would become Fort Lesley McNair—and remained there for 20 years. (LOC.)

This image shows the band marching along the parade field. Since the 3rd Cavalry's move with its band in February 1942, a section known as the "Funeral Band" was trucked to Arlington National Cemetery for performances at final honors. Finally, an "Advance Detachment of the Army Band" moved to Fort Myer on April 17, 1942. In June 1943, the prewar band was ordered overseas, while the auxiliary band remained at Fort Myer. Upon its return from overseas, the prewar band returned to Fort Myer, where it has been ever since. (TUSAB.)

The soldiers of 12th Infantry Regiment were stationed on the Arlington Cantonment until early 1941. In addition to defending the capital city, they provided ceremonial support for funerals at Arlington National Cemetery. In the upper image, Cpl. French L. Vineyard and squad are executing "port arms." All the men are members of Company M, 12th Infantry. Corporal Vineyard is wearing the new "pot-type" helmet. The other members of the squad are wearing the old "basin-type" helmet. In the lower image, soldiers of Infantry Squad Company M, 12th Infantry, are executing the "on guard" position and are prepared to do "long thrust" or "short thrust" with their World War I weapons. (Both LOC.)

The photographs above and below are street scenes of enlisted soldiers' barracks on South Post of Fort Myer. Barracks of this style were very common among all the camps and air bases that sprouted up around the United States during World War II (some bases were designated forts after the war, such as Fort Stewart, Georgia). Many of the ones on South Post would remain after World War II up to the early 1970s. They were easy to build and were needed to accommodate the millions of soldiers among the 90 divisions in Army Chief of Staff George C. Marshall's plan. (Both FMHO.)

The Women's Army Auxiliary Corps (WAAC) began on May 15, 1942, when Pres. Franklin D. Roosevelt signed the bill that Congress had passed the day before. Congress passed legislation that created a new branch of the US Army that became Women's Army Corps—WAC—on July 3, 1943. Nearly 2,000 of these women were stationed at South Post of Fort Myer, working in the Pentagon or other government agencies around Washington, DC. The images are on North Post of Fort Myer's parade field as the WAC officers proudly watch their soldiers pass in review. As a branch of the US Army, the Women's Army Corps would exist until 1975, and when dissolved, the soldiers would migrate into their "military occupational specialties"—MOS. (Both FMHO.)

By September 1945, World War II had been won; the Japanese had surrendered and signed the peace treaty agreement on the deck of the USS *Missouri*. Fort Myer became an "out-processing" center as soldiers were discharged from service. Here on the South Parade Field, discharge papers are presented as the US Army Band provides musical accompaniment for the men's departure. Across all services, 14 million served in World War II, among them 8.3 million in the US Army, and as the world heaved a sigh of relief, soldiers went back to being civilians and enjoying the freedoms for which they fought. (Both FMHO.)

Six

SHOWCASE FOR THE US ARMY AND THE NATION

After World War II, the US Army Band—"Pershing's Own"—came home to Fort Myer instead of Fort McNair. At Fort Myer, it resumed ceremonial duties in the Washington, DC, area—including funeral support at Arlington National Cemetery working with the Military District of Washington's Ceremonial Company of the US Army.

The need for a standing regiment to conduct the ceremonies and defend the capital was strong. Hence the 3rd Infantry was reactivated on April 6, 1948, with Col. Jesse B. Matlack as the first commander of the regiment. He would soon relinquish command to Col. James V. Cole. The Military District Washington Ceremonial Company became A Company in 1950.

On April 10, 1952, President Truman presented the regiment the Presidential Baton and named it "Honor Guard to the President." In 1953, the Guns Platoon—"Presidential Salute Battery"—was formalized to fire the 75-millimeter Field Gun Model 1897 (French)—the same gun that a National Guard Artillery unit used in World War I under the command of a future president, Capt. Harry S. Truman. The US Army Drill Team was organized in 1957. The Old Guard Fife and Drum Corps was organized in 1960. In 1963, the 3rd Infantry was officially recognized as "the Old Guard."

On the southernmost part of Fort Myer's North Post, the US Army Signal Corps erected a radio transmission station near the "Three Sisters." Station WAR was the cardinal point in the US Army's message network during World War II. The lower photograph shows the robust electronics of the day, which were developed and produced for the Army by Radio Corporation of America (RCA). Utilizing the capabilities of the "Three Sisters," the Army was able to communicate with the commanders in the field. Despite the removal of the three radio towers, the station continued after World War II as a way to keep tabs on communications from the embassies within the area. (Both NARA.)

Retiring from the US Army as one of the generals of the Army and Army chief of staff, Dwight D. Eisenhower and his wife "Mamie" get a "five-star" send-off as he leaves Fort Myer and the Washington, DC, area for only a short time. He headed to New York City to become president of Columbia University. Little did he know that he would soon return to Washington, DC, as president-elect of the United States of America. (Both FMHO.)

In 1946, Army Band commander Lt. Col. Hugh Curry and Capt. Samuel R. Loboda formed the US Army Band Chorus—a volunteer group of "Pershing's Own" instrumentalists who could sing—to fulfill Curry's wish for "a band with plenty of showmanship that not only plays well, but also sings well." The demand for the group was so great that designated singers needed to be selected to perform the missions for which the Army Band Chorus had been tasked. Because of this, on August 14, 1956, Secretary of the Army Wilbur Brucker established the US Army Chorus with 40 singers, plus pianists. (NARA.)

The Army Band spent 20 years located at what would become Fort McNair within the District of Columbia. Here is highlighted the tuba section of what would become the premier ceremonial orchestra within the US Army. (NARA.)

It is only fitting that the oldest infantry regiment in the US Army be its elite ceremonial unit. Nearly 100 years earlier, Gen. Winfield Scott had given them the name the "Old Guard of the Army." On April 6, 1948, in a ceremony on the US Capitol steps, the colors of the regiment were uncased, and the soldiers were given a dual mission of guardians of the US capital and the official ceremonial unit of the US Army. Col. Jesse B. Matlack became the first commander of the reactivated 3rd Infantry Regiment, and Col. James V. Cole then assumed command of the Old Guard from July 1948 to 1950. Soldiers selected to serve in the Old Guard have been through basic training, followed by extensive and specialized training with the 3rd Infantry. In the image above, Pfc. Joseph Lindgren is welcomed by Maj. Gen. Hobart R. Gay, commanding general of the Military District of Washington. (Both TOGM.)

Col. James V. Cole
1948 - 1950

The US Army regularly rotates its officers to provide them and the soldiers in their command enrichment and broadening of experience and skills. In 1948, Col. James V. Cole became the next post commander of Fort Myer and commander of the 3rd Infantry Regiment, relieving Col. Jesse J. Matlack—who just months before, as Fort Myer post commander, had participated in the reactivation and had assumed command of the regiment. (FMHO.)

Each year, the various units within the US Army celebrate "Organization Day." It is the day when the regiment remembers its beginnings and celebrates its long and proud history. It is a family day with events planned and perhaps a parade. Here, these "Fort Myer Cheerleaders" are celebrating the 165th birthday of the reactivated Old Guard—the 3rd Infantry Regiment. In 1949, there were installation sports teams, so these cheerleaders also cheered for the teams the post fielded. (FMHO.)

These images taken in 1949 show little change in North Post except for a parking lot and baseball field near the parade field, which would change over the years, as the drill field would no longer be needed. Buildings would soon spring up that would replace the area where cavalry and field artillery soldiers exercised their horses and honed the skills of war. The image below of South Post shows the Pentagon in the upper right and the buildings of this Lower Post still intact and occupied. As the need to expand Arlington National Cemetery grew, the buildings would be razed and disappear, only to become the final resting place for those who may have once walked the streets of the post. (Both NARA.)

Standing on Whipple Field, this image was taken in May 1949. Washington, DC, is seen with its memorials, monuments, and federal buildings dotting the landscape and providing a wonderful view of the city. Still the high ground and still defending the capital, Fort Myer is the opportune place to have a military installation. It is also the reason that US Army Signal Corps considered it a prime location for the Signal Corps School. (LOC.)

Military aviation began at Fort Myer in 1908. Fifty years later, many would gather on the same parade field where the Wright Flyer made its historic flight that September. A monument marking the event was erected. Seen here from left to right are Air Force Secretary James H. Douglas, Mrs. Frederic G. Kellond, Maj. Gen. Frank P. Lahm (USA Ret.), and the Hon. Hugh M. Milton II, acting secretary of the Army. Kellond was the sister of Lt. Thomas Selfridge, who was the first aviation fatality. (FMHO.)

In the 1950s, this is how the Henry Gate entrance to Fort Myer appeared. It was guarded by a soldier from the military police. It would provide access to the post from what would eventually become US Route 50. Familiar landmarks, including the motel, which still exists, are in the background on the left. (FMHO.)

Final honors for the fallen continue through the flawless execution of the US Army Band and the 3rd Infantry. These images show the band leading the procession, followed by formations of Old Guard soldiers. By the size of the procession, the final honors pictured here are for a flag officer, with a soldier bearing the officer's flag immediately following the caisson with its matching horses. The soldiers walking alongside pay honors to the one who served to defend the freedoms as they proceed to their final resting place. The traditions continue, just as they did years before when the cavalry and field artillery units provided the same dignified and respectful honors. (Both TOGM.)

Many final honors begin on Fort Myer, with the Old Post Chapel being the departure point for this outstanding way of honoring the fallen. The Old Guard, which is stationed here, still maintains a stable of horses who are groomed and kept in the tradition of days long gone. The caisson and its complement of soldiers riding the horses give a small suggestion of the thousands of each that occupied the post or even the US Army at one time. The lower image shows the famous Blackjack, a caparisoned (riderless) horse with the boots turned backward—a tradition suggesting that a leader would never ride again. The soldier walks the horse in the procession following the caisson. As a distinction, the caparisoned horse is reserved for those who have served in US Army and Marines with rank of colonel and above, horse cavalrymen, and anyone killed in action (KIA). (Both TOGM.)

Over time, the ceremonial duties of the US Army's 3rd Infantry and the US Army Band have continued to expand to include Department of the Army retirements and change-of-command and dignitary arrival/departure ceremonies either on what now is called Summerall Field, named after the 12th chief of staff of the US Army, or Whipple Field, overlooking Washington, DC. Both ceremonial units have grown in size and specialty as the needs of the US Army have continued to change. The upper image includes a presentation of the Old Guard's American Revolution–era origins. The Continental Color Guard is dressed in Continental Army uniforms. Each of the soldiers equipped with a rifle has a bayonet fixed, done in a small part of the ceremony to remind all that the members of the US Army's 3rd Infantry Regiment, "the Old Guard," march with their bayonets fixed at the end of their weapons. The lower image is the ceremonial band of the US Army Band. (Both TOGM.)

Added in 1960 to the US Army's 3rd Infantry Regiment, the Old Guard Fife and Drum Corps passes in review for its first-ever parade on April 21, 1960. The corps would go on to march in Revolutionary War–period uniform in every inaugural parade since Pres. John F. Kennedy's. Within the ranks are also a section of soldiers carrying bugles. The US Army is the only service branch which still uses the valveless instrument, especially when rendering Taps at final honors. (TOGM.)

Part of the Old Guard, assembled in formation, awaits the arrival of the dignitary it will honor that day. On the far right is the Old Guard Fife and Drum Corps in its Colonial-period uniforms. The drum major, standing in front of the soldiers, wears a distinctive hat and carries a spontoon as a sign of his rank. The spontoon is used to provide the members of the unit visual signals of the orders of movement and sequences to play. (TOGM.)

FIRST GUARD, TOMB OF THE
UNKNOWN SOLDIER IDENTIFICATION
BADGE AWARDED
AWARDED TO
MSG WILLIAM E. DANIEL
ON 7 FEBRUARY 1958

One of most elite units within the Old Guard contains the sentinels who guard the Tomb of the Unknown Soldier within Arlington National Cemetery. The first Unknown Soldier was interred in 1921; the first military guard was established at the tomb on March 25, 1926. When the US Army's 3rd Infantry was reactivated in 1948, this distinctive duty was assigned to a platoon within the Old Guard. Here, the sergeant of the guard marches his men past the reviewing party in a change-of-command ceremony. Note that on the sentinels' right pockets is the Tomb Guard Badge—one of the rarest badges issued in the US Army. The first badge was issued in 1958. As of 2010, less than 600 of these badges have been earned and issued. Tomb Badge No. 1, shown at left, is part of the Old Guard Museum collection. (Both TOGM.)

During the Cold War—especially in the 1950s—America continually demonstrated its might and powerful resources. The 3rd Infantry was no exception; it had a unit of M41 "Little Bulldog" tanks. They complemented the other tactical skills of the regiment and made very good shows at ceremonial events. Fortunately, they were never needed to defend the capital city, though they provided a powerful deterrent against outside forces. (TOGM.)

Even with an outstanding pair of parade fields on Fort Myer, the weather sometimes forces ceremonies to be held indoors. The riding arena no longer has a dirt floor, and the rafters are decorated with parachutes and flags from each of the United States. Departing Secretary of the Army Wilber M. Brucker is seen here "trooping the line" during an indoor review for him in January 1961. The US Army Band building at Fort Myer was later named for him. (FMHO.)

The US Army Drill Team was formed in 1958 as part of the 3rd Infantry Regiment. In the top image, this unique unit is on the Fort Myer Parade Field, and the color guard is in the center behind them. The several missiles in the background are Cold War displays of US military might. The image below shows one of the complex, demanding, and hazardous maneuvers that the drill team performs. Unique in its delivery, the US Army Drill Team has become known worldwide. (Both TOGM.)

Formed in 1953 as the Guns Platoon (also known as the Presidential Salute Battery), this elite unit fires the traditional 21-gun salute for the president or visiting heads of state. It also renders salute honors for certain flag officers at events, gives final honors, and announces the arrival of dignitaries who are to place a wreath at the Tomb of the Unknown Soldier. The image above, captured around 1960 after the gun salutes were rendered, was taken at what was then called Military Air Transport Service (MATS) at National Airport. (TOGM.)

This image was taken on Whipple Field with the platoon's guns facing to the east and the battery staff, along with each gunner and loader, standing proudly in front of its World War II–era M5s—three-inch antitank guns. Despite its artillery facing toward the nation's capital, it is part of the defenses of the city. The soldiers in this unit are carrying on the tradition of the field artillerymen of the field artillery units that preceded them years earlier at Fort Myer. Since they are infantrymen and are trained in indirect fire tactics, their specialty is mortars. (TOGM.)

DISCOVER THOUSANDS OF LOCAL HISTORY BOOKS FEATURING MILLIONS OF VINTAGE IMAGES

Arcadia Publishing, the leading local history publisher in the United States, is committed to making history accessible and meaningful through publishing books that celebrate and preserve the heritage of America's people and places.

Find more books like this at
www.arcadiapublishing.com

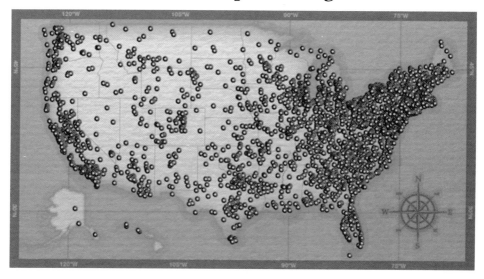

Search for your hometown history, your old stomping grounds, and even your favorite sports team.

Consistent with our mission to preserve history on a local level, this book was printed in South Carolina on American-made paper and manufactured entirely in the United States. Products carrying the accredited Forest Stewardship Council (FSC) label are printed on 100 percent FSC-certified paper.

MADE IN THE USA